# Mistakes and Heartbreaks
# Who knew God's Favorite would be Unfaithful?

A Self-Guided Journal

By: Amaris Potts

# Dedication

This book is dedicated to every faithful woman who has been cheated on. Hold your head up because God has amazing blessings for each of us.

And to Mr. Parker just as I began to realize at the end of writing this book that you and I were just pieces in his game of chess. I pray that you realize the same and know that God has something greater for you.

# INSPIRATION

I am inspired to write this journal after spending time completing the guided journey from my favorite waitress at Blu Rose named Janae Cheyenne and after being cheated on yet again in a relationship. Following my experiences, I don't want to harden my heart and wait another 5 years before I let another man in. So, I am hoping this book will help me heal and be a blessing to other women who have been cheated on. I started writing this book on November 27, 2021, when he left my house saying he thinks God is telling him I am not the person for him. It hurt even more because God told me clearly that he was the person for me. Even after God told me he cheated, He still insisted he was the one for me.

After he left, I prayed and asked God 'why would you tell me this if it's not true?' I thought, "Did He want to see if I would obey Him?" I have been more open in my personal life over the past few months than I have been in my entire adulthood and it's a wonderful feeling. Maybe others were right that we are not meant to be. Or maybe my test was to see if I would be obedient. I just can't seem to lay my hands on anything that may have triggered his actions but I will be praying for more answers. Also, I have been writing children's books and I just never seem to get it done. No matter how hard I try, I just keep getting stuck. But not this time. The words are flowing like water. I know this book was directed by God, but I'd wonder if my book will ever be published. I wonder if I should share this book with him before it's published. I still don't have the answers to that yet, but I know that by the end of my writing, God will give me a clear answer. Up to this day, I have love for him and God hasn't told me yet that he isn't the one for me. So, the purpose of this book isn't to bash but to bring healing. I hope if a copy gets to him, he will feel the same. Who knows, maybe this book is still part of God's Plan for us. Let's begin.

# A Praying Aunt

For I know the plans I have for you, declares the LORD, plans for welfare and not for evil, to give you a future and a hope

-Jeremiah 29: 11

It was after Christmas and Bella and I were at her aunt's house for one of our typical holiday visits. We live in a town where my ex-husband's family is also our family. You know, the pick up gifts, drop off gifts, and catching up on life visits. I'll never forget hearing

"And Amaris I have been praying that God sends you a good man." I was like, "Wait what?" This was a little shocking because I had been divorced since 2016 and separated since 2014. At the time, I had not been praying for a man. And I thought Bella was all I needed. Meanwhile, I'd crack a few jokes every now and then asking where is that stepdaddy when I know the cost of having a child would be a lot, but I wasn't praying for a man. Well, I was not faithfully praying on my knees each night for one because I was I-N-D-E-P-E-N-D-E-N-T. You know what that means. You must love that song.

What are some things others are praying for on your behalf? Do you ever wonder why you didn't pray for something yourself?

# The Beginning

*And after you have suffered a little while, the God of all grace, who has called you to his eternal glory in Christ, will himself restore, confirm, strengthen, and establish you.*

-1 Peter 5:10

After about a month, I eventually met a man. However, I met his daughter first before finally meeting him after a few weeks. We met because our children got parts in the Black History Program at our church. I didn't know much about him but he was the State Teacher of the Year. We had this one Deacon who wouldn't let us forget. I remember him and his family joining the church while I was already a member. I knew his wife had passed and that he was involved in the youth department. I sat on the front row watching the practice when he and his children walked in. At the time, I thought all three were his because I would always see the kids together. As the children walked up the steps to the stage, he stopped in front of me. I moved my belongings and welcomed him to sit next to me, and that was the start of our first interaction and what was to follow next.

Can you remember your first interaction with someone you loved? Describe the interactions. How did it make you feel?

As the kids practiced, we began to talk. Then, he told me that only two of the three were his and the other was his nephew. As we were still conversing, he mentioned that he would leave once his daughter begins to speak because she was usually shy around him. It was just a normal parent conversation and I didn't think much of it.

Following that interaction came a Facebook friend request and liking of my pictures. At first, I didn't think much of it because we had just met and I kind of had this rule not to date anyone who attended my church. Yeah I know, look at where not following that rule landed me. I just didn't want any drama, so I had turned down other advances in the past with the help of Bella. I'll never forget that one drummer who asked me my name in the lobby of the church and after I told him my name was Amaris, Bella looked at him and told him, "But you can call her Ms. Potts!" That moment was priceless.

Most women have a list of dating don'ts. What is on your list and think back to the time when you didn't stick to that list. How did it work out for you?

_____
_____
_____
_____
_____
_____
_____
_____
_____
_____

It was Sunday March 3, 2019, and for some reason, he was in the main sanctuary and not with the children at the end of church service. He sat on my side of the church. Yeah, I am one of those people who sits in the same area each Sunday. He was where the ushers sat until the end of service. Then it happened. He came up to me and told me he wanted to talk to me for a second. I just knew he was going to ask me to help with the youth department, so I was preparing a nice way to say no. His church best friend had already asked me several times for the same favor, so I was already convinced I knew his request. However, it turned out to be that he just wanted to let me know I was remarkably beautiful. And that was all he said. I said thank you and we stood there for a few moments of silence. Oh boy, it was awkward. I was used to men saying more before I shut them down. But he didn't say anything else. So, I told him I needed to go find Bella. I thanked him and walked away.

As I drove home, I thought about his very few words. I must admit it was a little weird, but it gave me butterflies. A few hours after church, I noticed a Facebook message from him that said "Don't know if my words today were out of place. If so, I hope you will forgive me." I let him know his words were not out of place. It just wasn't what I thought he was about to say. The Facebook conversation carried on that evening with him wanting to know more about me. I explained to him that the majority of my time was spent with Bella and I loved music, food, and movies. And that I was hoping to add travel in the next two years. On October 11, 2021, God made a way for me and I accepted a job that allows me to travel.

He went on to explain to me that he doesn't really get to do what he wants to do because he has a lot of things he does with his twins, work, and speaking engagements. He told me he liked Bruno Mars, Mariah Carey, Jay Z, and Outkast. While we were dating, he told me a story of a famous rapper he was cool with who came to Fort Valley to perform a few times and that he got on stage. He was very proud of this moment and told me this same story three times. This conversation went on for about two days. I let him know I like Regulars by Warren G, Grillz, and the Ghost Town Djs. At the end of the second day of keeping in touch, he asked me to meet for lunch.

I now wonder if we should have spent more time talking before we went on a date. Could spending more time behind the computer or on the phone build that friendship I missed in my marriage and in this relationship? I believe so. I think we should have just been friends the first year. Sometimes, I look back to couples who have been married for years. I discovered that when they tell their stories, they will say 'we grew up together or we were friends for a long time.' I see this is a common mistake I have been making. I believe it's a mistake he also is making, but he has to realize that for himself. **Mistake Number One.** If we could start over today, I would first build the relationship on friendship.

How long were you friends with your boyfriend/spouse or ex before you started dating? If you could change the time frame, would you? Explain?

# Our First Lunch Date

May the God of hope fill you with all joy and peace as you trust in him, so that you may overflow with hope by the power of the Holy Spirit. Romans 15:13

Since we worked and lived in different cities, I was shocked that he could travel to my city to have lunch with me. When he arrived, we met at Little Hawaiian, one of my favorite places to eat in Carrollton, Georgia. We got into a conversation to share our experiences and know each other better. Well, he talked for over an hour and I listened to every word. I found him very intriguing and highly intelligent. He talked about the Bahamas, the places in Carrollton he had visited, and his career. We even talked about him turning 40 that year on May 9. He would later find out the crazy look on my face when he told me his birthday, was because it was the same as my ex-husband's. Maybe this was a red flag, but I found myself wanting to learn more.

Can you remember your first date? Where did you go and what did you wear? How did it make you feel? I had on a grey dress and he had on a suit with a bow tie. He had called ahead to reserve a table for the two of us.

# BETTER TIMES

I have found the one whom my soul loves.

Song of Solomon 3:4

Over the next few months, we got closer. We went on more dates. Our second date was at Gabe's in Villa Rica. This was the night he kissed me. I was a little shocked because things seem to be moving quite fast, but he was winning my heart. He was saying all of the right things, and it felt good to talk to someone besides my child at night. I was starting to see how much I had missed over the past 5 years. We talked every day. Each night when we would get off the phone, he would say "sweet dreams." We both made time for each other and he introduced me to so many new places. I had told him I loved food, so we would go to restaurants I had never been to in Atlanta and Douglasville. One afternoon, we ventured to Newnan when he was in a nearby town for a work trip. We enjoyed debating each other. I would question his comments, which made him rethink what he said. I believe I opened his eyes to see other points of view. His first trip while we were getting to know each other was in Chicago and he invited me to join him. I declined because I had Bella and it seemed a little strange. At first, I thought maybe he was just being sweet, but he continued to invite me on each trip he took. So, I knew this was important to him.

He was such a gentleman. He would open doors for me and won't let me pay for anything. This was our first mini disagreement. I never wanted him to feel like he had to pay for everything, but I would offend him when I tried to pay.

Eventually, we talked about this and listened to each other's reasoning. For him, this was what he was taught by his grandmother who raised him. For me, I was used to paying in my previous marriage. Undeniably, it felt good not to have to be the breadwinner. I had never had this feeling before. I never dated a man who was more successful than I am. So, this experience was all new to me.

What role did you play in your previous relationship? What role did your ex play? How did it affect your relationship?

_____
_____
_____
_____
_____
_____
_____
_____
_____
_____
_____
_____
_____
_____
_____
_____
_____
_____
_____
_____
_____
_____

At this time, we had not told anyone we were dating. I now realize this was **Mistake Number Two** for us. See, I had always been a private person. Since we attended the same church, I think he didn't want anyone to think we started dating while his wife was still alive. I say this because he had once told me that when word get out that we are dating, he would always protect me. At the time, I had no clue what he was talking about because we did nothing wrong. So, we both had our reasons and at the time they made sense, but when I look back, it was a mistake.

We had some really great times together, from being foodies together to watching his friend's play at Clark Atlanta University to even going to see his favorite comedian of all time, Dave Chappelle. We both got our very first couple massages together at Serenbe in Chattahoochee Hills. It was beautiful. I thought our cooking class at Chateau Elan was great, but this place was breathtaking. We went back several times to see Joanna and Heather. But my favorite times together were when we prayed. Before each dinner we prayed. When parentings was hard we prayed. When pulling out of the driveway we prayed.

What were some positive experiences with you and your boyfriend/spouse /ex?

_____
_____
_____
_____
_____
_____
_____
_____
_____
_____
_____
_____
_____
_____
_____
_____
_____
_____
_____
_____
_____
_____

# Moving in the Right Direction. Well, I thought

*Fear not, for I am with you; be not dismayed, for I am your God; I will strengthen you, I will help you, I will uphold you with my righteous right hand. Isaiah 41:10*

For the first time in years, I felt safe. His home felt like my home. We had talked about my divorce and I had told him how my ex cheated on me. He promised me he would never cheat nor hurt me, and I believed him. That was **Mistake Number Three**. This was the same line my ex told me. My past fear was marrying a man who had many women like my dad. Yes, my papa was a rolling stone and I have over 25 brothers and sisters. I shared this with my ex-husband and he promised not to cheat as well. I really wish they both would have said they would try their best not to hurt me. At least maybe that would have made things better for me mentally.

My summers at this time were really busy with work, but we would still make time for each other. I would stop by later when the kids were asleep and we would often watch Jeopardy or Triple D. We would even watch movies. One of his favorite movies was Love Actually. Since he didn't like me driving home late at night, I would sleep over and just leave before the kids woke up. Things were going in the right direction. Or so I thought. I realize now that things moved way too fast and we didn't build a friendship.

On July 30, 2019, I was making plans to go over to his house the following night. Prior to this, we had planned to hang out the week before. Bella would be with her dad and this was the first time I would be able to go over since the turn (A horrible time of year to anyone in the student housing industry) had started. I will never forget the sadness that came over me when he told me he would have to prepare the kids for tomorrow because it was the day their mom passed. I understood and prayed for him and the twins. I knew his wife had passed but I wasn't sure when. I later realized that this was the one-year anniversary of her passing.

The following night, I came over to his place and this was the first time we had a deep conversation. I told him I didn't realize it had not been a year since his wife passed and then asked him if he was sure he was ready to date. For me, I had been separated and divorced for 5 years and he was the first person I dated. He explained to me that everyone heals differently. He assured me that he was fine and was ready to move forward. He had grieved and was ready to date. **Mistake Number Four**. He was not ready and I felt like God was trying to tell me when he put it on my heart to ask him about it. But I listened to the man. Maybe had we waited, our ending would have been different.

How long before ending one relationship do you start another one?

I was learning a lot about him, but he wasn't learning as much about me because he talks for the most part during our conversations and I wasn't a very open person. And, I ask a lot of questions. Every question I have usually comes with a follow-up question, but he didn't ask questions like me. There were times when I would be trying to tell him things and he would cut me off with his thoughts. I never thought he did it on purpose; he just is a speaker and he loves to talk. Oftentimes, I would ask him to stop talking so I could talk.

One night, as we sat in his room after watching Jeopardy, he asked me what would be our next steps. I made him understand that it will be spending more time with the kids. It was important to me that he got to know Bella and I got to know his kids as well. So, we started spending more time with the 5 of us. It was really great. He and Bella connected quickly because they both are people persons. Also, his daughter and I connected. I believe she looked at me as being fun and funny. And his son loved giving me hugs and rubbing my hair. When we were with the kids, we showed no affection to each other. They didn't know we were dating. They thought we were just friends hanging out. Those times were really good. I prayed that times would go back to these later in the relationship, but the relationship ended before that could happen.

# THE IN-LAWS

A fool gives full vent to his spirit, but a wise man quietly holds it back. Proverbs 29:11

Since he had no blood family in this area and his parents were in the Bahamas, his in-laws basically helped him out a lot. I understood this because just like him, I had no blood family here and my in-laws helped me. At this time, his mother in-law worked in the same building as him. I remember seeing her for the first time one afternoon when I dropped him off back to work from one of our many lunch dates. I would take days off during the week when I could and pick him up for lunch.

Now, this is the story he told me. I wasn't there. One afternoon, she walked down to his office and closed his door. She said to him, "Would you like to tell me about Amaris?" He said he was stocked and short with her. **Mistake Number Five.** Why were we hiding our love? Yes, we planned on telling the kids first, then the world. But the kids were talking about the fun we were all having together and people started to figure it out. We even had a few church members figure it out because of the way we looked at each other in Bible study. He was told he gave me a glow. This is why it's so hard to hear another woman say he gave her a glow. To me, I felt that was my glow and how could he make two women glow?

That December, as Bella and I were shopping for a tennis racket and balls, he called to ask if we wanted to have dinner. So, he and the kids came to Carrollton and we met at Shane's. I vividly remember this moment like yesterday. His daughter was talking and told me her cousin said I was the devil and he wanted to come up with a plan to get rid of me.

Of course, my protector, Bella, was furious. I calmed her down, then replied to the comment and apologized that he felt that way, reiterating that it would change with time. Well, I don't feel it ever changed.

Do you have in-laws? How is your relationship with your in-laws?

_____
_____
_____
_____
_____
_____
_____
_____
_____

I could tell he was embarrassed by the comment and he said he would be speaking to his nephew's parents. For me, I knew I was being talked about in that home by the adults for the child to make comments like that. It was hurtful and sad because they never got to meet me and never took the time to learn about me. I guess I could have done the same but it's hard to be around people who don't like you just because you aren't their family member who passed away. Maybe it was too soon for them to welcome a new person. I know now it was too soon for him. Or maybe it was because I was not in the education field like the rest of the family.

I told him it was okay that he didn't have to tell them about the comment. I knew he needed them to help with the kids and I didn't want to mess up his support team. I was willing to be talked about and hurt if it meant him having the help he needed. Truth is, I should have never felt this way. He made it seem like his in-laws didn't matter. To the very end, he still made it seem this way. After having a very deep conversation about his marriage at the end of our relationship, it all made sense. There is a hold they have over him and they are influencers in his decisions. I know he will never agree to this, but it's the truth. It's hard to change something that has been going on for 17 years. My prayer for him is that one day, he sees it.

# The Pandemic

*There will be great earthquakes, famines and pestilences in various places, and fearful and great signs from heaven. Luke 21:11*

Right before the pandemic, we decided to tell our kids we liked each other. We each talked to our own kids separately about how we felt for each other. All three were excited. His daughter even wanted to help him plan dates for me and told him to take me to my favorite places. Here, we made **Mistake Number Six.** Yes, we needed to tell the kids, but we also should have told the kids together. We were already in love, and we should have shown the kids how we felt . I think out of all the mistakes, this very one hurts the most. We continued to spend time together as a family and it felt great. Our one-on-one time was declining due to him not wanting his in-laws to keep the kids and them not really wanting to keep the kids either. These were his words. I never met them and I never talked to them. We still had our late nights where I would travel to his house when Bella was away. We even planned a Spring Break cruise but it was canceled due to the pandemic.

Did any of your plans change in 2020 due to the pandemic? Did you lose or gain any friendships? Did you start a new hobby?

_____
_____
_____
_____

For a few months, we didn't see each other because we were staying home due to Covid. We would still talk daily and things were still good between the five of us. Once the pandemic let up, we started back from where we left off. But this time, our interactions in front of the kids were different. We missed each other dearly that we would hold hands, he would lay his head on my lap, and we would sit closer to each other on the sofa. In one of such moments, I noticed his daughter would come to sit between us or if a part of his body was touching me, she would move his body. I told him I thought she missed her mom several times and he said yes. He noticed her change when I am around.

This continued for months and I constantly told him what I was seeing. But he kept saying he was going to talk to her. I had been joining him and the kids for dinner even when I didn't have

Bella. I was doing this before the pandemic and both kids enjoyed our time together. But after the pandemic, I noticed that only one seemed to like me being around without Bella. This broke my heart. I felt alone and didn't feel like he was helping enough to salvage the situation. He kept saying he was going to talk to her, but he never did. **Mistake Number Seven.** I should have talked to her. This hurts me even to this day. Why didn't I step up and talk to her?

As I replayed our relationship in my mind over the past few months, I realized I was still holding on to a comment he made about Bella the weekend of July 4th. Bella was only playing with a little boy in his neighborhood. There were 4 other kids around but she was only playing with him. He told me he thought Bella liked his little neighbor. I didn't see it, so I was like "really?" He said yes, he can tell. So, I suggested that maybe he should talk to her. He said, "She isn't my child." **Mistake Number Eight** These words hurt me so bad. I carried this hurt for the remainder of our relationship and he never knew until the end. This was one of the reasons I believe my relationship with his daughter stopped growing, and I didn't think at the time his daughter needed me. We talked about this a few weeks ago. He said he remembered saying this but didn't know why he said it and he apologized.

In your current or past relationships, have you ever said something you regret? How did you handle it? Does it still hurt you today?

# A Gift from My Mom

*Every good and perfect gift is from above, coming down from the Father of the heavenly lights, who does not change like shifting shadows -James 1:17*

It was Christmas time and my mom who had never met his kids already loved them and treated them like her grandkids. Any holiday Bella got a card, they did as well. I was meeting my sister in January 2021 to give her some items to give to my mom since my mom was at her house. Well, to my surprise, my mom came with her. So, we ended up having brunch and she gave me his kids Christmas gifts. Since I wasn't too far from his house, I decided to stop by so the kids could get their gifts. I think this was a huge turning point in our relationship. His daughter opened the door and was so cold to me. That was the coldest she had ever been to me. I handed him the cards and left. He followed me to the car asking if I was okay. He could see I was hurting and about to cry. For months, I had been telling him that she missed her mom and he did nothing about it. My heart hurt because I loved and still love them to this day. I was so emotional that I cried the entire way home.

He called and asked me if I was okay. He said he could tell I was about to cry when I walked out of his house. He then told me that he knows she missed her mom but didn't know what to do. Then, he highlighted that I needed to spend time with her and I felt like she needed him at this time. She wasn't ready to spend one-on-one time with me. The timing was not right and I didn't want to force myself on her. I tried to tell him about this but he didn't listen. He videoed a conversation with him and her and it hurt me even more. In the video, I saw her telling him over and over again that she doesn't want to go anywhere with me without Bella. Because he kept asking, she started to change her answers and wanted to only go to the Waffle House down the street with me. To this day, he never knew how much this hurt and he still doesn't see at this moment that she needed him and not me. I do believe some one-on-one time with him first would have been the start to her healing before she would begin to spend time with me. We both failed her.

Are there times in your relationship that you feel you are not heard? How does/did it make you feel?

I told him I would step back and stop coming around until she felt more comfortable because I could see the pain in her eyes whenever I was there. It was a reminder that her mom was not there. He asked me what I would do if I was in that situation. I told him that I would simply say, "I notice having Ms. Amaris around reminds you of mommy not being here. We want to respect you so Ms. Amaris will not come around as much until you are ready." I told him I would also make sure she understood that we were still going to be friends and would still be spending time together without them. **Mistake Number Nine.**

After giving him advice he asked for, he told me "Well, how would you know what you would do because you are not in this situation?" This hurt so much because I had given him so much advice in the past, from helping improve his relationship with his mom, morning routines, to preparing for the week ahead of time, and even the way he continued to have her do things because she moves just a little faster than his son. And now he has an issue with the advice he asked me for. This pain never went away for me because we never talked about it. Moving forward, whenever he would ask for advice, I would say I am not in that situation so I can't speak about it. This was wrong and I never should have said that.

How do you make step-parents feel like they are important too when it comes to parenting?

_____
_____
_____
_____
_____
_____
_____
_____
_____
_____
_____
_____
_____
_____
_____
_____
_____
_____
_____
_____
_____
_____
_____

# DISTRACTIONS

Blessed is the one who perseveres under trial because, having stood the test, that person will receive the crown of life that the Lord has promised to those who love him. When tempted, no one should say, "God is tempting me." For God cannot be tempted by evil, nor does he tempt anyone; but each is tempted when they are dragged away by their own evil desire and enticed. James 1 12-14

As time progressed, 2021 started to become worse and worse for me. Not only were we having issues in our relationship and not communicating correctly, I continued to have issues at work. It was stressful and took up much of my time. After a few months, he told me that his daughter is now okay with me being around without Bella. Note that he never asked me how I felt. Maybe if he had asked, I would have told him I don't feel comfortable right now. Why the change? Was this a true change? How did she heal? I know I had not healed from the time I left his house crying. And in my heart, I knew she wasn't ready too. So, I declined invites to join the three of them without Bella. **Mistake Number Ten.** This opened up time for him to spend with Ms. Parker and her two daughters. But I knew his daughter wasn't ready for him to be in a relationship.

As I became more unhappy at work, I noticed it was affecting our relationship, and all of our conversations was about my work. So, I stopped complaining to him about work because I didn't want my complaints to weigh him down. Gradually, we began to drift apart. He was no longer available for one-on-one time. And because I wanted more and got tired of only coming over at night, it all kind of paused. He wasn't the same guy I met in February 2019. The guy who sent me flowers to brighten my day. The guy who made time for me. The guy who called me beautiful. The entire time, I thought it was my work-life balance.

I was applying for jobs all through the night and on weekends as I tried to find a job that would make my life better so I could be the girlfriend I knew he needed and deserved. All this time, I didn't know there was someone else. I never knew about Ms. Parker. It wasn't until November that I found out his time with her started well before our time ended. It was heartbreaking. Imagine thinking for months that you were the reason a relationship didn't work out, only to find out he started engaging with another woman in February. To find out he couldn't attend the church we share, but supported her on the front row of her church and sat with her parents. It really hurt.

He was spending more and more time on his phone during the little times we managed to spend together. We continue to spend time together over the summer by taking the kids to the water parks and on a trip to Tampa. There were some good moments and bad moments but to me, that is part of having kids. I never knew that while he was dating and spending time with me, he was also dating her and having the kids around her. I'm sure they were confused. Maybe they were even told not to say anything about Ms. Parker around me. Who knows?

What were some of your distractions in your last relationship?
_____
_____

# Our Ending

And we know that in all things God works for the good of those who love him, who have been called according to his purpose.

Romans 8:28

My busy time of year was starting and I was already drowning at work and our relationship was sinking. My mom had come to help me like she always does, but this time, she had to stay several extra days because I was breaking down. This entire time, he was not by my side and I guess it was because I spent a lot of time at work and he was with Ms. Parker.

Two days after the students moved in, I applied for a work-from-home position. I knew this was the job for me and God told me it was mine. Could this be the answer to my prayers? It was a remote job, so I thought to myself that I could help him more. I could work from his home on some days. I could try to rebuild what was breaking. On my first free weekend after working a month straight with no days off, I reached out to him. I wanted us to talk. I knew he was traveling that month to see his mom but I didn't recall the date. It happened to be that same weekend. I didn't want to put a damper on his trip, so I told him to enjoy himself. I told myself that next weekend would be better to talk since Bella would be with her dad. I wanted to talk about work and our relationship and the changes that were about to happen.

God told me I would be getting this job. God told me to leave my current job on August 16. That night I cried and I prayed because I was scared. I was scared to quit my job with no start date for a new job. But that job I was currently on was affecting me mentally. It was hurting my relationship with him and all three kids. The morning of August 17, 2021 I called my mom, crying and telling her I was putting in my notice. I couldn't do it anymore. I called her because I knew I would need financial support. I didn't want to tell him because I didn't want him to talk me out of it. We had had this conversation before and it brought it no result. My plan was to tell him after I put in the notice so there would be no turning back at that point.

As I sat at my desk waiting for my computer to start, I started opening mail. We had a FedEx package that I figured was vendor checks, but I noticed it was more, so I opened it. It was a handmade cup holder and a Bible scripture Psalms 37:23-24. I began to cry harder. It had no name on it but I knew who it was from. As tears rolled down my face, I began to email her thanking her and letting her know I was about to put in my notice because it was just too much and that the job was affecting me mentally and my personal life. She told me she knew I was having a hard time and that she will always be there for me. This was the role he used to play in my life but we were drifting apart. I was trying to hold my tears so I could write the notice, and I knew the staff would start coming in and I didn't want to create a scene if they notice I have tears in my eyes.

Then that is when it happened. He dumped me via text message on August 17, 2021. The tears started flowing again. The text made no sense at all. He said we tried everything. What was he talking about? We hadn't had a real conversation in weeks. We never talked. We did not try everything. The text was a complete lie. I was hurt and heartbroken but I didn't let him know.

**Mistake Number Eleven.** For months, I regretted not telling him what was going on with me that day. It was until last week that I really thought maybe it would have been different if he had known. But now, I know it wouldn't have been. He was not coming to our church, instead he attended her church and sat with her mom while still in a relationship with me. The kids had already been introduced to her. He had already emotionally detached himself from me and was attached to her. He had already been intimate with her while in a relationship with me. I lost my guy to the mistress, Ms. Parker.

At the time, I didn't know anything about her. It wasn't until November 11, 2021, the truth started to come out. Yes, at this time we were no longer in a relationship, but I knew in my heart that he had started dating her before ending things with me. This book isn't to tell you all my experiences or to bash either of them. This book is to help me and others heal. This book is to help us focus on the mistakes that can be made in a relationship. You know God works in mysterious ways. And I said in November, God has a plan for this pain.

Our last moments, on November 27, 2021, was hard. A year ago, I had purchased a journal for Bella that says 'To my Daughter.' I had the journal for an entire year and picked it up a few times but never wrote in it. The journal's purpose was to have positive messages in it for her and the day she graduated, it would be a gift to her. I wanted her to have something to hold on to if she ever felt alone.

Last week, it occurred to me why I had not written in the journal. When I purchased the book, I was supposed to purchase three. So, I ordered one for his son and one for his daughter with plans to do the same for them. His daughter's journal came in while I was out of town and was one of the many packages he brought with him when he arrived at my house. I told him the story and handed him the journal. He looked down as tears flowed from my very pretty face. I had on makeup from family pictures Bella and I took. He asked to give me a hug and I declined as he walked out of my door one last time. Well, I thought it was the last time.

He told me he thinks God is telling him I am not the one and I accepted that even though it hurt me so bad and I could tell he wasn't being truthful. He has a tell when he is not beining truthful that I discovered early this month. My prayer for him is that he takes time to himself and learn to love himself. Above all, he should always be there and caters for his kids. He said God hasn't answered him about Ms. Parker, but I could tell by the look on his face that wasn't true. I could tell he was going to continue with her that night and he was still not being truthful.

In 2019, he told me I was the answer to his prayers, but now in 2021, she was the answer to his prayers. I do wish him the best of luck. I still believe that God would never give a woman a man who is already in a relationship. And I still believe that relationships built on lies will not work out and are not favored by God. Though in my home, he agrees with these statements. And told me several times I that I was correct. He believes God wouldn't do this as well. Then he says something different after he speaks to Ms. Parker. Can it be both?

My ex-husband lied to me when we met. It wasn't until after we were married that I found out our relationship was built on lies.

And I could share so many stories that support what I am saying, but those aren't my stories to tell.

I know for a fact that building friendship will be first thing I must do before starting my next relationship. And who knows maybe when the time is right, God might bring us back together. God has told me to wait on him. God revealed that the man he is today isn't the man for me, but the man he will become is.

# And Then There Was More

*Consider it pure joy, my brothers and sisters, whenever you face trials of many kinds, because you know that the testing of your faith produces perseverance. Let perseverance finish its work so that you may be mature and complete, not lacking anything.*
James 1:2-4

I thought this book was over, but there's more to it. Well, today is December 23, 2021, and I wrote the parts of this guide you just read a month ago. I knew this book was from God because the words flowed so easily for me last month, but I stopped. I stopped because of the love I had for a man and I didn't want to move forward with this book because I didn't want to hurt him. I didn't want to move forward because God told me he wanted us to use this painful situation to bless others. I was waiting so we could be the author of this story together. But clearly, from his harsh text, that is not the case. I will not wait to complete my assignment from God. I will use this painful situation to try my best to help others who have had to deal with this pain. Maybe one day, he will no longer be afraid and use his mistakes to help others. Even with all the pain he has caused me, I was still trying to protect his image. But the one above, the one I call Father, told me the world needs this book.

I don't want to hurt him, but his text tonight was the confirmation from God that this book needs to be finished and it's not about him, but about HIM. He said God told him I was strong. This is the only thing I believe is true from everything he has said over the past two months. I am strong and I will be just fine.

You see, I knew he wasn't taking the advice he said our pastor gave him. That was to take time to be alone. I knew his flesh picked Ms. Parker even when he said God had not answered him on November 27, 2021.

I am not the first woman to be cheated on by a minister. Sad to say, I know I will not be the last. I am sure there are many others dealing with being cheated on by a man of God right now. I regret holding him to a higher standard because of his title. I now realize he is just like every other man I dated. Weak!

It hurts to know so many men came to him in their time of need, confessing that they were cheating on their partners. It hurts that he had no compassion for them and was doing the same as them. It hurts to have heard him say his cheating was different because we aren't married. Really bruh?

It hurts to have told him how my ex-husband brought his mistress to our church and sat right beside me with her. It hurts to have told him that my ex also told me he never loved me. You know why it hurts? Because his reply to me was, "Those things are way worse than what I did to you." He told me in his last text that while in a relationship with me, he was praying that God would bring him someone else. WOW! Truly, he had become a self-centered coward. For two months, and countless three hour conversations never did he say any of this to me. Was he upset because of the letter I send to Ms. Parker? Was he afraid that now that she knew what he has been telling me, she would see him for who he really was? Was he afraid she would be upset to find out he has just vistied my home that week? I can only imagine the lies he must have told her about me.

It hurts that my child had to witness me being hurt and is too young for me to tell her the truth. It hurts that he hurt her by hurting me and has no care in the world about the pain he has caused in my home.

It hurts that I waited 5 years before giving someone a chance and ending up this way.

It hurts to finally hear God clearly and the same person God tells me is for me doesn't hear the same and has treated me and my child like we are nothing.

It hurts to know that there may be a day when a man treats his daughter the way he treated me and the kids have to suffer from the actions of their parents. You see, karma doesn't always just come for you. It comes for the ones you love the most.

It hurts to be left confused once again and to have wasted years with someone who gave you hope.

What are some things in your past relationship that still hurts you?

_____
_____
_____
_____
_____
_____
_____
_____

When I started this journey, God gave me a few words. The first word was 'humble', then 'open', then 'obedient', and then 'pride'. I am currently obedient. Every task God has given me, I have completed from reading, writing and even visiting a grave. All the things I know I would have never done on my own. I'm so proud of the progress I have made to be the Best Me possible.

It's funny because he used to tell me all the time "Amaris, I only know how to be me." I asked him if this is still true in our last communications and he didn't reply. Well, let me take that back. I blocked him so I wouldn't know if he replied or not.

To you my dear ex, I hope you finally learn who you are and be that person, because clearly, you know how to be many people. I forgave you when I knew the truth before you admitted it to me, because as I told you last month, God revealed it to me.

And to Ms. Parker, I pray that God sends you "your guy", a man who will not build a relationship on lies. One who has enough respect for the queens you and the girls are. I know you desperately want to be married. Over the past month, he and I had many conversations about you and we talked about your past. We share similar stories as he liked to keep telling me. I saw my ex-husband get remarried, have more kids, shoot that joker even purchased a house in Mirror Lake. The place he wanted our second home to be. There was a time I asked God why He would reward him when he did wrong. Why him and not me? But I think this is where our stories took different paths. For me, God wanted me focus on my child, not finding a new husband. When He told me you had dated several people since your divorce, it then clicked. This is where our paths differ. Many blessings to you.

And my prayer for me is that God removes every image of this man from my mind, heart, and head. I did everything you asked of me. Lord, I pray that I wake up in the morning with a message from you saying I no longer have to wait on him. I want better and I deserve better. My child deserves better. Don't harden my heart. Don't put hate in my heart for him. Because I know you want me to love everyone. Amen

# What I learned about myself from this relationship?

Let love and faithfulness never leave you; bind them around your neck, write them on the tablet of your heart. Then you will win favor and a good name in the sight of God and man.

Proverbs 3:3-4:

- Friendship - If we had a friendship, the relationship would have had a better chance of working. We would have had a foundation. This didn't come to me until the night he left my house for the next to the last time and I started writing this book. Taking my time in my next relationship and building that friendship first will lead to everlasting love.

- Communicating - This is an area I am weak in. I don't do a really good job expressing my feelings. My communication style is passive-aggressive and I need to be assertive. This isn't something I can do on my own, so I need a therapist to help me improve in this area. I want to be open and I want to express myself with the person I am with.

- Forgiveness: I realize when I don't talk about pains and hurts, I don't give myself the opportunity to forgive. Talking about the pains and hurts with the person who hurt me is important for forgiveness. I was holding on to pain because we never talked about it. But after we talked and he apologized, I can honestly say it was forgiven.

- Seek Help: We needed help a long time ago. All of the signs were there. Not having a support group of God-loving couples is damaging. For my next relationship, it's important for me that we have couples to talk to.

- Variety: I need variety in my relationship. I need things to stay fun and exciting. I am not a roach.

- Significance: We both need to feel important and our jobs, life happenings, or kids should never be a reason for not spending time together.

- Growth: A more real conversation about growth is needed from the start. I now see that a relationship is a job. And for your job, you have to have bi-yearly evaluation. This should be done in a relationship as well.

- Worthy: My child and I are both worthy of someone who would never hurt us. We deserve better and God has something better in store for us. His blessings are overflowing. No woman, not even Ms. Parker deserves an unfaithful, disconnected, untrustworthy, and flesh-driven man.

- Keep God First: It's important for me that the next man who comes into our lives is a true believer. I just can't deal with weak men anymore who run from God and relationships when times are hard. I can't be with a man who talks to single friends about problems, leaving out big parts of the problem like "man I am cheating" just to get the answer he wants to hear. I want a man who will take our problems to God while I do the same, and then we go to God together. I want a man who is committed as I am. A man who will love me to the end of time.

As for what God is telling me about him, I can't answer that today. You see I made a promise to try my very best to never disobey God again. So I stopped praying for him and about the situation. I know this might not be right, but for now it works for me. If I don't pray about it, then I cant hear what God has to say about it. I don't want to hear God say wait on him, so I've decided for now to block him out of my life.

And God did answer me about sharing my books with him. I did not share either of my books with my ex before being published. He made his choice and I made mine to turn this pain into a purpose. I pray the women and men reading my book know they are not alone.

What did you learn about yourself in your past or current relationship?

_____
_____
_____
_____
_____
_____
_____
_____
_____
_____
_____
_____
_____
_____
_____
_____
_____
_____
_____
_____
_____
_____
_____
_____
_____
_____
_____

Be kind to each other, tenderhearted, forgiving one another, just as God through Christ has forgiven you. **Ephesians 4:32**

Made in the USA
Columbia, SC
31 July 2022